Introduction:

Welcome to "Mastering TikTok Ads: Unlocking the Power of Viral Marketing." In this comprehensive guide, we will explore the world of TikTok advertising and equip you with the knowledge and strategies you need to create effective and successful ad campaigns on one of the most influential social media platforms today. Whether you are a marketer, entrepreneur, or business owner, this ebook will take you through the ins and outs of TikTok ads, helping you harness its immense potential to reach millions of users and drive tangible results for your brand.

Chapter 1: The Rise of TikTok Advertising

Understanding the explosive growth of TikTok and its unique audience demographics.

Understanding the explosive growth of TikTok and its unique audience demographics is crucial for successful advertising on the platform. TikTok has experienced remarkable growth, becoming one of the most popular social media platforms worldwide. Here are key points to consider:

1. Global Reach: TikTok has a vast global reach, with over 2 billion downloads worldwide and an active user base spanning multiple countries. It has gained significant popularity among younger demographics, particularly Gen Z and Millennials.

2. Demographics: TikTok's audience demographics skew towards younger users. It has a strong presence among teenagers and young adults, with a large portion of its user base falling within the age range of 16 to 24. However, the platform's popularity is gradually expanding to include older age groups as well.

3. Creative Culture: TikTok fosters a unique creative culture that encourages users to express themselves through short-form videos. The

platform's emphasis on creative content and entertainment has contributed to its rapid growth and engaged user base.

4. Viral Potential: TikTok's algorithm and content discovery mechanisms make it conducive to viral content. This means that well-crafted and engaging videos have the potential to reach millions of users and gain significant visibility.

5. Diverse Interests: TikTok's user base encompasses a wide range of interests and niches, including music, dance, comedy, beauty, fashion, DIY, and more. This diversity presents ample opportunities for advertisers to connect with specific target audiences.

6. Global Influencer Network: TikTok boasts a vast network of influencers who have gained substantial followings and influence on the platform. Collaborating with these influencers can help amplify brand messaging and reach a wider audience.

Understanding these factors can guide advertisers in tailoring their ad campaigns to resonate with TikTok's unique audience demographics. By embracing the creative culture, targeting the right demographics, and leveraging the platform's viral potential, advertisers can maximize their impact and drive successful outcomes on TikTok.

Exploring the advantages of advertising on TikTok compared to other platforms.

Advertising on TikTok offers several advantages compared to other platforms. Here are some key advantages to consider:

1. Growing User Base: TikTok has experienced exponential growth in its user base, with millions of active users worldwide. This presents a significant opportunity to reach a vast and diverse audience, particularly younger demographics such as Gen Z and Millennials.

2. High Engagement: TikTok users are highly engaged with the platform, spending an average of 52 minutes per day on the app. This level of

engagement provides advertisers with ample opportunity to capture users' attention and deliver their brand message effectively.

3. Creative and Authentic Content: TikTok's emphasis on creative, short-form videos allows for authentic and engaging content. Advertisers can leverage this format to create unique, entertaining, and memorable ads that resonate with the platform's user base. This creative freedom can lead to increased brand awareness and user engagement.

4. Viral Potential: TikTok's algorithm is designed to promote viral content, increasing the chances of ads reaching a broader audience. Well-crafted ads have the potential to go viral and gain widespread visibility, resulting in increased brand exposure and potential organic reach.

5. Influencer Collaboration: TikTok boasts a thriving community of influencers who have amassed substantial followings. Collaborating with relevant influencers allows advertisers to tap into their influence, credibility, and engaged audience, amplifying brand reach and generating authentic user engagement.

6. Targeting Capabilities: TikTok offers advanced targeting options that allow advertisers to refine their audience reach based on demographics, interests, and behaviors. This level of targeting precision enables advertisers to deliver their ads to specific segments, increasing the likelihood of reaching the right audience for their products or services.

7. Lower Competition: Compared to more established advertising platforms, TikTok's advertising ecosystem is still evolving, meaning there is relatively lower competition. This can present opportunities for early adopters to gain a competitive edge and achieve better ad performance.

While it's important to consider the advantages, it's also crucial to align your advertising goals and target audience with the specific strengths and demographics of TikTok. By understanding these advantages, advertisers can leverage TikTok's unique features and user base to create impactful ad campaigns and achieve their marketing objectives.

Overview of the various ad formats available on TikTok.

TikTok offers several ad formats that allow advertisers to engage with users in different ways. Here's an overview of the various ad formats available on TikTok:

1. In-Feed Ads: In-Feed Ads appear in users' main video feed and blend seamlessly with organic content. They typically appear as short videos and can include various elements such as images, text, and call-to-action buttons. In-Feed Ads allow advertisers to create immersive and engaging experiences for users.

2. Brand Takeovers: Brand Takeovers are full-screen ads that appear when users open the TikTok app. They provide high visibility and instant exposure to the advertiser's brand. These ads can include images, videos, or GIFs, and they typically link to a landing page or an in-app hashtag challenge.

3. TopView Ads: TopView Ads are similar to Brand Takeovers but have an extended duration. When users open the TikTok app, TopView Ads are the first content they see, providing maximum impact. Advertisers can leverage this format to showcase their brand message with longer videos or more detailed content.

4. Branded Hashtag Challenges: Branded Hashtag Challenges are an interactive ad format that encourages user participation. Advertisers create a branded hashtag and challenge users to create and share content related to the challenge. This format generates user-generated content, increases brand visibility, and fosters user engagement.

5. Branded Effects: Branded Effects allow advertisers to create custom AR (augmented reality) effects, stickers, and filters that users can apply to their videos. These effects are associated with the advertiser's brand and can enhance brand recognition, engagement, and virality.

6. Branded AR Content: Advertisers can collaborate with TikTok to create bespoke AR experiences, games, or filters for users to interact with. This

format provides a unique and immersive way to engage users and aligns the brand with innovative and interactive content.

7. Influencer Partnerships: In addition to the official ad formats, advertisers can collaborate with TikTok influencers to promote their products or services. Influencer partnerships can help leverage the influencer's existing audience and authenticity to deliver branded content in a more organic and relatable manner.

Each ad format offers distinct advantages and can be tailored to specific campaign objectives and target audiences. Advertisers can experiment with different formats to find the most effective and engaging ways to connect with TikTok's user base and achieve their advertising goals.

Chapter 2: Setting Up Your TikTok Ads Account

Step-by-step guide to creating a TikTok Ads account.

Here is a step-by-step guide to creating a TikTok Ads account:

1. Visit the TikTok Ads Manager: Go to the TikTok Ads Manager website (ads.tiktok.com) and click on the "Create an Ad" button.

2. Sign up or Log in: If you already have a TikTok account, you can log in using your existing credentials. If you don't have an account, click on the "Sign Up" button to create a new account.

3. Choose Account Type: Select your account type. You can choose between "Business Account" if you're promoting your own business or "Personal Account" if you're an individual advertiser.

4. Enter Account Details: Provide the necessary information to set up your account, including your email address, password, and country/region.

5. Verify Your Email: TikTok will send a verification email to the email address you provided. Go to your email inbox, find the verification email,

and click on the verification link to complete the email verification process.

6. Set Up Your Profile: After email verification, you'll be prompted to set up your profile. Fill in the required details such as your account name, profile picture, and other relevant information.

7. Create an Ad Campaign: Once your profile is set up, you can start creating your first ad campaign. Click on the "Create" button in the TikTok Ads Manager dashboard to begin.

8. Choose Campaign Objective: Select your campaign objective, such as brand awareness, app installs, website traffic, or conversions. Choose the objective that aligns with your advertising goals.

9. Define Campaign Settings: Set the campaign name, budget, duration, ad delivery optimization, and schedule. These settings determine how your ads will be displayed and optimized.

10. Create Ad Groups: Within your campaign, create ad groups to organize your ads based on targeting, budget, or other criteria. Specify the targeting options, budget allocation, and bidding strategy for each ad group.

11. Design Your Ad Creative: Create your ad creative by uploading images or videos, adding text overlays, captions, and call-to-action buttons. Follow TikTok's guidelines for ad creative specifications and best practices.

12. Set Targeting Options: Define your target audience based on demographics, interests, behaviors, or custom audiences. TikTok offers various targeting options to help you reach your desired audience effectively.

13. Set Bid and Budget: Determine your bid strategy and set your daily or lifetime budget for the campaign. You can choose between automatic bidding or manual bidding, depending on your preference.

14. Review and Launch: Review all the campaign settings, targeting options, and ad creative before finalizing your campaign. Make any necessary adjustments, and once you're satisfied, click on the "Launch" button to start running your ads.

15. Monitor and Optimize: After launching your campaign, regularly monitor its performance using the TikTok Ads Manager dashboard. Analyze the key metrics and make data-driven optimizations to improve the effectiveness of your ads.

By following these steps, you can successfully create a TikTok Ads account and start running your ad campaigns on the platform. Remember to familiarize yourself with TikTok's ad policies and guidelines to ensure compliance and optimize your advertising efforts.

Navigating the TikTok Ads Manager interface and understanding its features.

Navigating the TikTok Ads Manager interface is essential for managing and optimizing your advertising campaigns effectively. Here's an overview of its main features and how to navigate through them:

1. Dashboard: The TikTok Ads Manager dashboard is your main hub for managing your campaigns. It provides an overview of your account's performance, including key metrics, spending, and ad groups.

2. Campaigns Tab: The Campaigns tab displays all your active, paused, and completed campaigns. You can view the performance metrics of each campaign, make edits, duplicate campaigns, or create new ones.

3. Ad Groups Tab: The Ad Groups tab allows you to manage individual ad groups within your campaigns. Here, you can view metrics specific to each ad group, adjust targeting options, budgets, and bids, and monitor performance.

4. Ads Tab: The Ads tab lists all the ads you have created. You can track their performance, make changes, pause or resume ads, and access individual ad settings.

5. Creative Library: The Creative Library is where you can manage and organize your ad creative assets. You can upload images, videos, and other media files, create new ad templates, and preview or edit existing creatives.

6. Audiences: The Audiences section enables you to create, manage, and organize custom audiences for targeting. You can create audiences based on user engagement, website visitors, or uploaded customer data to enhance your ad targeting capabilities.

7. Reporting: TikTok Ads Manager provides comprehensive reporting tools to analyze your campaign performance. You can generate customizable reports, review key metrics, and export data for further analysis.

8. Billing: The Billing section allows you to manage your payment methods, view your billing history, and access invoices. You can set up automatic payments, update billing information, and monitor your account's financial aspects.

9. Account Settings: In the Account Settings, you can manage your account details, such as your contact information, time zone, and notification preferences. It is also where you can manage team member access and permissions.

10. Help Center and Support: If you need assistance or have questions, the TikTok Ads Manager interface provides access to the Help Center and support options. You can find useful resources, FAQs, and contact support for further assistance.

When navigating the TikTok Ads Manager interface, familiarize yourself with its features and functionalities to efficiently manage your campaigns, monitor performance, and make data-driven optimizations.

Regularly explore the various tabs and sections to leverage the platform's tools and insights for effective advertising on TikTok.

Best practices for account setup and optimization.

Setting up and optimizing your TikTok account is crucial for building a strong presence on the platform and maximizing your reach and engagement. Here are some best practices to follow:

1. Choose a Relevant Username: Select a username that aligns with your brand or business. Keep it concise, memorable, and easy to spell. Avoid using numbers or symbols that may confuse users.

2. Complete Your Profile: Fill out your profile with relevant information. Add a profile picture that represents your brand, write a catchy and informative bio, and include links to your website or other social media accounts if applicable. A well-rounded profile helps users understand your brand and encourages them to engage with your content.

3. Consistent Branding: Maintain consistent branding across your TikTok account. Use similar colors, fonts, and visual elements in your profile picture, cover image, and video content. Consistency helps users recognize your brand and builds trust and familiarity.

4. Engaging Profile Description: Craft an engaging and concise profile description that clearly communicates your brand's value proposition. Highlight what sets you apart and why users should follow or engage with your content. Be creative, compelling, and use relevant keywords.

5. Post High-Quality Content: Create high-quality, visually appealing videos that align with your brand and resonate with your target audience. Pay attention to video resolution, lighting, and audio quality. Use editing features, effects, and filters to enhance the overall visual experience.

6. Be Authentic and Entertaining: TikTok thrives on authenticity and entertainment. Focus on creating content that is relatable, engaging, and entertaining for your target audience. Experiment with different video

formats, trends, challenges, and storytelling techniques to keep your content fresh and engaging.

7. Leverage TikTok Trends: Stay updated with the latest trends, hashtags, and challenges on TikTok. Incorporate relevant trends into your content to increase your visibility and connect with the broader TikTok community. However, ensure that the trends align with your brand values and target audience.

8. Engage with the TikTok Community: Actively engage with other TikTok users by liking, commenting, and sharing their content. Respond to comments on your videos and foster a sense of community and interaction. Engaging with others helps build relationships, increase visibility, and attract more followers.

9. Utilize Hashtags Wisely: Use relevant and popular hashtags in your video captions to increase discoverability. Research trending and niche-specific hashtags related to your content and industry. However, avoid overusing hashtags or using irrelevant ones, as it may come across as spammy or inauthentic.

10. Analyze and Optimize: Regularly review your TikTok analytics to understand which types of content perform well and resonate with your audience. Pay attention to metrics such as views, likes, shares, and engagement rates. Use this data to optimize your content strategy, identify trends, and refine your approach.

11. Collaborate with Influencers: Consider partnering with TikTok influencers who align with your brand. Collaborations with influencers can expand your reach, tap into their engaged audience, and lend credibility to your brand.

By following these best practices, you can set up a compelling TikTok account and optimize your content strategy to drive engagement, attract followers, and achieve your marketing goals on the platform.

Chapter 3: Defining Your Objectives and Target Audience

Identifying your advertising goals and aligning them with the capabilities of TikTok Ads.

Before diving into TikTok Ads, it's crucial to identify your advertising goals and ensure they align with the capabilities of the platform. Here's a step-by-step process to help you in this alignment:

1. Define Your Advertising Goals: Start by clearly defining your advertising goals. Are you aiming to increase brand awareness, drive website traffic, generate leads, boost app installs, or increase conversions? Having well-defined goals will guide your advertising strategy on TikTok.

2. Understand TikTok's Target Audience: Familiarize yourself with TikTok's user demographics and understand if they align with your target audience. TikTok primarily appeals to younger demographics, such as Gen Z and Millennials. If your target audience falls within these age groups, TikTok can be a suitable platform for your advertising goals.

3. Explore TikTok's Ad Formats: Review the various ad formats available on TikTok and determine which formats best align with your advertising goals. For example, if you want to create brand awareness and engagement, In-Feed Ads or Branded Hashtag Challenges can be effective options. If you aim to drive app installs, consider utilizing App Install Ads.

4. Consider Creative Requirements: Evaluate whether your creative assets, such as images or videos, meet TikTok's creative requirements. TikTok emphasizes creative and visually appealing content, so ensure your assets are optimized for the platform and can capture users' attention within seconds.

5. Assess Targeting Capabilities: Understand TikTok's targeting capabilities and determine if they can effectively reach your desired audience. TikTok offers options to target users based on demographics, interests, behaviors, and even custom audiences. Assess if these targeting options align with your audience segmentation needs.

6. Budget and Cost Considerations: Determine your budget and consider the cost of advertising on TikTok. Evaluate whether the cost aligns with your advertising goals and if you can allocate sufficient resources to achieve meaningful results on the platform.

7. Measure and Track Results: Consider how you will measure and track the performance of your TikTok Ads campaigns. TikTok provides analytics and reporting tools within the Ads Manager to monitor key metrics and evaluate campaign effectiveness. Ensure you have the capability to track and analyze the results to optimize your campaigns accordingly.

8. Iterate and Optimize: Keep in mind that advertising on TikTok may require experimentation and optimization. Continuously monitor your campaign performance, make data-driven adjustments, and iterate your strategies to maximize your desired outcomes.

By aligning your advertising goals with the capabilities of TikTok Ads, you can effectively leverage the platform's features and reach your target audience while achieving your desired outcomes.

Conducting thorough audience research to define your target audience on TikTok.

Conducting thorough audience research is crucial to define your target audience on TikTok effectively. Here's a step-by-step guide to conducting audience research for TikTok:

1. Understand Your Existing Customers: Start by analyzing your existing customer base. Look at demographic information such as age, gender, location, and interests. Identify any patterns or commonalities among your customers to get an initial understanding of your target audience.

2. Analyze TikTok User Demographics: Research TikTok's user demographics to understand if they align with your target audience. TikTok primarily attracts younger demographics, particularly Gen Z and Millennials. Consider if your products, services, or brand resonate with these age groups.

3. Utilize TikTok's Audience Insights: TikTok offers an Audience Insights tool within the TikTok Ads Manager. Utilize this tool to gain valuable insights into TikTok's user behavior, demographics, interests, and device usage. Explore the data to identify potential segments that align with your target audience.

4. Conduct Surveys and Interviews: Conduct surveys or interviews with your existing customers or target audience to gather firsthand insights. Ask questions about their TikTok usage, content preferences, and interests related to your industry. This qualitative data can provide valuable insights into their motivations and behaviors on the platform.

5. Analyze Competitor Audiences: Research your competitors' TikTok presence and audience. Analyze the type of content they produce, engagement levels, and the demographics of their followers. Identify any gaps or opportunities in reaching a specific segment of the audience that might be relevant to your brand.

6. Leverage Social Listening Tools: Use social listening tools to monitor conversations and trends related to your industry or relevant topics on TikTok. This can help you understand what content resonates with your target audience, their preferences, and the language they use.

7. Engage with TikTok Communities: Engage with TikTok communities, including relevant hashtags and challenges, to observe the conversations and interactions. Pay attention to the content creators, influencers, and popular trends within these communities to gain insights into your target audience's interests and preferences.

8. Analyze Analytics and Performance Data: Once you start running TikTok Ads, analyze the performance data within the TikTok Ads Manager. Look at metrics such as engagement rates, click-through rates, and conversions to understand which segments of your audience are responding positively to your ads.

9. Refine and Iterate: Continuously refine and iterate your target audience based on the insights gained from your research and campaign data. As

you gather more data and feedback, adjust your targeting parameters to optimize your ad campaigns and better reach your desired audience.

By conducting thorough audience research on TikTok, you can gain a deep understanding of your target audience's demographics, behaviors, and preferences. This information will enable you to create more targeted and engaging content, tailor your advertising strategies, and maximize your success on the platform.

Utilizing TikTok's targeting options to reach your desired audience effectively.

Utilizing TikTok's targeting options is crucial to reach your desired audience effectively. Here are some key targeting options available on TikTok Ads that you can leverage:

1. Demographic Targeting: TikTok allows you to target users based on demographic factors such as age, gender, location, and language. Define the specific demographics that align with your target audience to narrow down your targeting and reach the right people.

2. Interest-Based Targeting: TikTok enables you to target users based on their interests and preferences. You can select from a wide range of interest categories and subcategories to align with your product or service offerings. This helps you reach users who are more likely to engage with your content.

3. Behavioral Targeting: TikTok provides behavioral targeting options that allow you to reach users based on their past behaviors on the platform. You can target users who have interacted with specific TikTok content, engaged with certain types of ads, or completed specific actions. This targeting helps you reach users with demonstrated interests relevant to your brand.

4. Custom Audience Targeting: Utilize TikTok's custom audience targeting feature to reach specific groups of users. You can create custom audiences by uploading customer lists, remarketing to website visitors, or

targeting users based on their app activity. Custom audience targeting helps you reach users who have already shown interest in your brand.

5. Lookalike Audience Targeting: TikTok offers lookalike audience targeting, which allows you to expand your reach by targeting users who have similar characteristics and behaviors to your existing customer base. This targeting option helps you find new potential customers who are likely to be interested in your offerings.

6. Device and Network Targeting: TikTok enables you to target users based on the devices they use, including mobile devices, tablets, or specific operating systems. You can also target users based on their network connection, such as Wi-Fi or cellular data. This targeting option helps optimize your ads for specific device types or network conditions.

7. Retargeting: With TikTok's retargeting feature, you can reach users who have already engaged with your brand or visited your website. By retargeting these users with relevant ads, you can increase the chances of conversion and drive them further down the sales funnel.

8. Exclusion Targeting: TikTok also allows you to exclude specific audiences from seeing your ads. This can be useful if you want to refine your targeting further and exclude users who may not be relevant to your campaign objectives.

When utilizing TikTok's targeting options, consider combining different targeting criteria to create a comprehensive and tailored approach. Continuously monitor the performance of your ads and adjust your targeting parameters based on the insights you gather to optimize your campaign effectiveness.

Remember, effective targeting on TikTok requires a deep understanding of your target audience and aligning the available options with your specific campaign goals.

Chapter 4: Crafting Compelling TikTok Ad Campaigns

Creating captivating ad content that aligns with TikTok's creative culture.

Creating captivating ad content that aligns with TikTok's creative culture is essential to engage users and make a lasting impact. Here are some tips to help you create compelling ad content on TikTok:

1. Embrace Authenticity: TikTok users appreciate genuine and authentic content. Embrace the platform's creative culture by creating ads that feel natural, relatable, and unpolished. Avoid overly polished or overly promotional content that may come across as inauthentic.

2. Leverage User-Generated Content (UGC): UGC is highly popular on TikTok. Consider incorporating UGC elements into your ads to tap into the user community and foster engagement. Encourage users to create and share content related to your brand or products, and showcase their creations in your ads.

3. Short and Snappy Format: TikTok thrives on short-form content. Keep your ad content concise, attention-grabbing, and to-the-point. Capture users' attention within the first few seconds and deliver your message quickly to maximize engagement.

4. Incorporate Trends and Challenges: TikTok is known for its trends and challenges. Stay up-to-date with the latest viral trends and challenges on the platform and find creative ways to incorporate them into your ads. This helps your content feel current, relatable, and connected to the TikTok community.

5. Use Music and Sound Effects: TikTok is heavily driven by music and sound effects. Incorporate catchy tunes, popular songs, or relevant sound effects into your ads to create a more immersive and engaging experience. Choose music that resonates with your target audience and enhances the overall mood of your content.

6. Experiment with Creative Effects: TikTok offers a wide range of creative effects, filters, and stickers. Experiment with these features to make your ads visually appealing and stand out from the crowd. Be mindful of the effect's relevance to your message and use them in a way that enhances your ad's impact.

7. Focus on Storytelling: TikTok provides an opportunity to tell compelling stories. Craft narratives or story arcs within your ad content to captivate viewers and keep them engaged. Develop a clear beginning, middle, and end to your ad, and use storytelling techniques to evoke emotions and create a memorable experience.

8. Call-to-Action (CTA): Incorporate a clear and compelling call-to-action in your ads. Prompt viewers to take the desired action, whether it's visiting your website, downloading an app, making a purchase, or engaging with your content. Make the CTA prominent and easy to follow.

9. Test and Iterate: Continuously test different ad variations, creative approaches, and messaging to identify what resonates best with your target audience. Analyze the performance metrics and gather insights to refine and optimize your ad content over time.

Remember, TikTok's creative culture is dynamic and constantly evolving. Stay tuned to the latest trends, user behaviors, and emerging content formats to keep your ad content fresh, relevant, and engaging.

<u>**Understanding the elements of a successful TikTok ad, including music, effects, and storytelling.**</u>

To create a successful TikTok ad, it's important to understand and leverage key elements such as music, effects, and storytelling. Here's a breakdown of each element and how they contribute to the success of your TikTok ads:

1. Music:

Music is a central component of TikTok's culture and can greatly impact the success of your ad. Consider the following when incorporating music into your TikTok ad:

- Choose Catchy and Popular Songs: Select songs that are popular on TikTok or have a catchy melody to capture users' attention and make your ad more memorable.

- Reflect the Mood and Tone: Use music that aligns with the mood and tone of your ad. Whether it's upbeat and energetic or sentimental and emotional, the right music can enhance the overall impact of your message.

- Use Music Transitions: Take advantage of TikTok's music transition feature to add an element of surprise or create seamless transitions between different scenes or shots within your ad.

2. Effects and Filters:

TikTok offers a wide range of effects, filters, and stickers that can add creativity and visual appeal to your ad. Consider the following when using effects and filters:

- Enhance Visuals: Experiment with different effects and filters to make your ad visually captivating. Use effects that enhance the colors, lighting, or overall aesthetics of your content.

- Reinforce Branding: Incorporate branded effects or filters that align with your brand identity. This can help create a consistent and recognizable visual style across your TikTok ads.

- Highlight Key Messages: Use effects strategically to highlight key messages or calls-to-action within your ad. This can draw attention to important elements and increase engagement.

3. Storytelling:

Storytelling is a powerful tool to engage and connect with TikTok users. Consider the following when crafting a narrative for your TikTok ad:

- Create a Hook: Start your ad with a strong and attention-grabbing hook within the first few seconds. This can be a captivating visual, an intriguing question, or an unexpected element that piques viewers' curiosity.

- Tell a Compelling Story: Develop a narrative or story arc within your ad that resonates with your target audience. This could involve showcasing a problem, presenting a solution, or taking viewers on an emotional journey that aligns with your brand or product.

- Show Real-life Scenarios: Use relatable scenarios or real-life situations that viewers can connect with. This helps build an emotional connection and makes your ad more relatable and memorable.

- Incorporate a Resolution: Conclude your ad with a satisfying resolution or a clear call-to-action that prompts viewers to take the desired next step, whether it's visiting a website, making a purchase, or engaging with your brand in some way.

Remember, a successful TikTok ad combines these elements in a way that is authentic, engaging, and aligned with TikTok's creative culture. Continuously analyze the performance of your ads, gather feedback, and iterate your approach to optimize the impact and effectiveness of your TikTok ad campaigns.

Tips for optimizing ad performance and maximizing engagement.

To optimize your TikTok ad performance and maximize engagement, consider the following tips:

1. Test Different Ad Formats: Experiment with various ad formats offered by TikTok, such as in-feed ads, branded effects, or top-view ads. Test different formats to see which ones resonate best with your target audience and drive higher engagement.

2. Optimize Ad Creative: Continuously refine and optimize your ad creative based on performance data. Test different visuals, captions, calls-to-action, and creative elements to identify what works best for your target audience. Monitor engagement metrics and make data-driven decisions to improve your ad content.

3. Keep Ads Short and Snappy: TikTok's platform thrives on short-form content, so keep your ads concise and attention-grabbing. Aim for ad durations that are around 15-30 seconds, focusing on delivering your key message quickly and effectively.

4. Capture Attention Early: Grab viewers' attention within the first few seconds of your ad. Use compelling visuals, intriguing hooks, or surprising elements to hook users and encourage them to watch the entire ad.

5. Use Captions and Text: Incorporate captions or text overlays in your ad content. Not all TikTok users listen to videos with sound, so adding captions can ensure your message is still conveyed effectively.

6. Leverage Influencers: Collaborate with TikTok influencers who have a relevant audience and align with your brand. Influencer partnerships can help you reach a wider audience and drive higher engagement, leveraging the influencers' existing rapport with their followers.

7. Encourage User Interaction: Design your ads to encourage user interaction and engagement. Prompt users to like, comment, share, or participate in challenges related to your brand. This can boost engagement and amplify the reach of your ads.

8. A/B Testing: Conduct A/B testing to compare different variations of your ads. Test different visuals, messaging, calls-to-action, or targeting options to identify the most effective combination. Use the insights gained from A/B testing to optimize your ad performance.

9. Monitor Performance Metrics: Regularly monitor and analyze key performance metrics, such as click-through rates, engagement rates,

conversion rates, and cost per action. Identify trends, patterns, or areas for improvement and adjust your ad strategy accordingly.

10. Optimize Targeting: Continuously refine and optimize your target audience based on performance data. Test different targeting options, narrow down your audience, or expand to new segments to find the most receptive audience for your ads.

11. Consistent Branding: Maintain consistent branding across your TikTok ads. Use consistent colors, logos, and messaging to reinforce brand recognition and build trust among viewers.

12. Seasonal and Trending Content: Stay updated with seasonal events, holidays, and trending topics on TikTok. Incorporate relevant themes or content into your ads to make them timely and resonate with users.

Remember, optimizing ad performance on TikTok requires continuous monitoring, testing, and adaptation. Stay informed about the latest platform updates, user behaviors, and trends to keep your ad strategy fresh and effective.

Chapter 5: Leveraging TikTok Influencers and User-Generated Content

Harnessing the power of TikTok influencers to amplify your brand's reach.

Harnessing the power of TikTok influencers can be a highly effective strategy to amplify your brand's reach and connect with your target audience. Here are some tips to make the most of TikTok influencers:

1. Identify Relevant Influencers: Look for influencers whose content aligns with your brand values, target audience, and campaign objectives. Research their follower demographics, engagement rates, and content style to ensure a good fit.

2. Set Clear Objectives: Define your goals for the influencer partnership. Whether it's increasing brand awareness, driving conversions, or boosting engagement, having clear objectives will help you choose the right influencers and measure the success of your collaboration.

3. Establish Authentic Partnerships: Seek influencers who authentically resonate with your brand. Look for those who genuinely use and appreciate your products or have a natural affinity for your industry. Authentic partnerships foster credibility and trust among their followers.

4. Engage in Meaningful Collaboration: Collaborate with influencers to co-create content that blends their unique style with your brand's messaging. Encourage creativity and allow influencers to express themselves while keeping your brand guidelines in mind.

5. Leverage Influencer Expertise: Influencers understand their audience better than anyone. Trust their expertise and allow them to provide insights and recommendations on how to effectively engage their followers. Collaborate on content ideas, captions, and calls-to-action to optimize the impact of your partnership.

6. Track Performance Metrics: Establish key performance indicators (KPIs) to measure the success of your influencer campaigns. Monitor metrics such as reach, engagement, click-through rates, conversions, and brand sentiment. Use tracking tools and affiliate links to attribute results to the influencer's efforts.

7. Long-Term Relationships: Consider building long-term relationships with influencers who consistently deliver results and align well with your brand. Long-term collaborations allow for deeper connections, increased familiarity with your brand, and ongoing engagement with their audience.

8. Leverage Challenges and Trends: Engage influencers in participating in popular challenges or leveraging trending topics on TikTok. This helps maximize exposure and aligns your brand with the current cultural conversation.

9. User-Generated Content (UGC): Encourage influencers to create user-generated content related to your brand. This can include product reviews, tutorials, testimonials, or creative content that highlights your brand's value. UGC generates authenticity and can inspire their followers to engage with your brand.

10. Amplify Influencer Content: Once influencers publish content featuring your brand, leverage that content across your own social media channels. Repost, share, or embed influencer content on your brand's TikTok account or other platforms to extend its reach and reinforce social proof.

11. Engage with Influencer's Audience: Monitor the comments and engagement on influencer posts featuring your brand. Respond to comments, answer questions, and engage with their followers. This demonstrates your brand's commitment and fosters a positive relationship with the influencer's audience.

Remember, building successful influencer partnerships on TikTok requires careful research, collaboration, and mutual trust. By leveraging the reach and influence of TikTok influencers, you can tap into their engaged audience and amplify your brand's visibility and impact.

Strategies for collaborating with influencers and creating authentic partnerships.

When collaborating with influencers and aiming to create authentic partnerships, consider the following strategies:

1. Identify the Right Influencers: Research and identify influencers who align with your brand's values, target audience, and campaign goals. Look for influencers who have genuine engagement, a loyal following, and produce high-quality content.

2. Establish Shared Objectives: Clearly communicate your campaign objectives and goals to the influencers. Ensure that they understand the

desired outcomes and align their content creation accordingly. This helps create a mutual understanding and a shared vision for the collaboration.

3. Emphasize Authenticity: Seek influencers who have a genuine interest in your brand or industry. Authentic partnerships are built on shared values and a natural affinity. Look for influencers who organically incorporate your brand into their content or have expressed interest in working with you.

4. Co-create Content: Collaborate with influencers to co-create content that blends their unique style with your brand messaging. Involve them in the creative process and provide them with creative freedom while ensuring the content aligns with your brand guidelines. This approach helps maintain authenticity and allows influencers to showcase their creativity.

5. Provide Value to Influencers: Offer influencers value beyond monetary compensation. This could include early access to products, exclusive discounts, or opportunities for unique experiences related to your brand. By providing additional value, you can strengthen the partnership and foster a long-term relationship.

6. Encourage Honest Reviews: Allow influencers to provide honest reviews and opinions about your products or services. Authenticity is crucial, and genuine reviews help build trust with their audience. Embrace constructive feedback and use it as an opportunity to improve your offerings.

7. Foster Long-term Relationships: Consider building long-term relationships with influencers who consistently deliver results and align well with your brand. Long-term collaborations allow for deeper connections, increased familiarity with your brand, and ongoing engagement with their audience. This also enhances authenticity and credibility.

8. Respect Influencer's Creativity: Recognize that influencers know their audience best. Trust their expertise and allow them creative freedom

within the agreed-upon guidelines. Encourage them to provide input, share ideas, and tailor the content to resonate with their followers.

9. Engage in Open Communication: Maintain open lines of communication with influencers throughout the collaboration. Regularly check in, provide feedback, and address any concerns or questions they may have. Building a strong working relationship based on effective communication helps ensure a successful partnership.

10. Measure Performance and Provide Feedback: Track the performance of influencer collaborations using relevant metrics and key performance indicators (KPIs). Measure engagement, reach, conversions, and other relevant metrics to evaluate the effectiveness of the partnership. Provide feedback to influencers to acknowledge their efforts and offer suggestions for improvement.

11. Be Transparent and Compliant: Ensure compliance with advertising guidelines and regulations. Clearly disclose any sponsored content or partnerships according to relevant advertising standards. Transparency builds trust with the audience and maintains ethical practices.

By implementing these strategies, you can cultivate authentic partnerships with influencers that benefit both your brand and the influencers themselves. Building trust, mutual respect, and shared goals are key to creating successful and meaningful collaborations.

Encouraging user-generated content to drive organic engagement and virality.

Encouraging user-generated content (UGC) is a powerful strategy to drive organic engagement and virality on TikTok. Here are some tips to encourage UGC and leverage it effectively:

1. Create a Hashtag Challenge: Launch a hashtag challenge that prompts TikTok users to create content related to your brand or a specific theme. Make the challenge fun, creative, and easy to participate in. Encourage

users to use your branded hashtag and share their videos, which will amplify the reach and engagement of your campaign.

2. Offer Incentives or Rewards: Provide incentives or rewards to users who participate in your UGC campaigns. This can be in the form of giveaways, discounts, exclusive content, or the chance to be featured on your brand's TikTok account. Incentives motivate users to engage with your brand and create UGC.

3. Showcase and Share UGC: Regularly feature and share UGC on your brand's TikTok account. Highlighting user-created content not only acknowledges and appreciates your audience but also encourages others to participate. This can inspire a sense of community and motivate users to create their own content.

4. Engage and Respond: Actively engage with users who create UGC related to your brand. Like, comment, and share their content to show appreciation. Respond to comments, answer questions, and foster a dialogue with your audience. This encourages further engagement and participation.

5. Collaborate with Influencers: Collaborate with influencers to create UGC around your brand. Influencers can generate high-quality content that inspires their followers to participate. Their endorsement and engagement can significantly boost the visibility and virality of your UGC campaigns.

6. Provide Clear Instructions: When launching UGC campaigns, provide clear instructions on what you want users to create. Specify the theme, content format, or specific elements you'd like to see. Clear instructions make it easier for users to participate and create content that aligns with your objectives.

7. Showcase UGC in Advertisements: Consider incorporating UGC into your TikTok ad campaigns. Authentic user-generated content can resonate well with viewers and generate higher engagement. By featuring

UGC in ads, you showcase real experiences and build social proof for your brand.

8. Run Contests or Challenges: Organize contests or challenges that revolve around UGC. Encourage users to submit their own videos, stories, or creative interpretations related to your brand or a specific campaign. Offer prizes or recognition for the best entries, motivating users to participate.

9. Share UGC Across Platforms: Extend the reach of UGC by sharing it across other social media platforms or your brand's website. Embed UGC videos on your website or share them on platforms like Instagram, Facebook, or YouTube. This widens the audience and increases the exposure of the UGC.

10. Engage with Trending Content: Stay aware of the latest TikTok trends and incorporate them into your UGC campaigns. Align your content with popular challenges, sounds, or formats that are currently trending. This increases the likelihood of your UGC going viral and gaining wider visibility.

Remember to always acknowledge and give credit to users who create UGC for your brand. By actively encouraging and leveraging user-generated content, you can tap into the creativity and enthusiasm of your audience, drive organic engagement, and enhance the virality of your brand on TikTok.

Chapter 6: Monitoring and Optimizing Your TikTok Ad Campaigns

Essential metrics to track and measure the success of your ad campaigns.

When tracking and measuring the success of your ad campaigns on TikTok, it's important to monitor various metrics to gain insights into their performance. Here are some essential metrics to track:

1. Impressions: Impressions measure the number of times your ad is displayed on TikTok. This metric indicates the reach of your campaign and how many users have potentially seen your ad.

2. Click-Through Rate (CTR): CTR is the percentage of users who clicked on your ad after seeing it. It helps determine the effectiveness of your ad in capturing viewers' attention and compelling them to take action.

3. Engagement Rate: Engagement rate measures the level of user engagement with your ad. It includes metrics such as likes, comments, shares, and saves. A higher engagement rate indicates that your ad resonates well with the audience and encourages interaction.

4. Conversion Rate: Conversion rate tracks the percentage of users who completed a desired action after clicking on your ad, such as making a purchase, signing up for a newsletter, or downloading an app. This metric measures the effectiveness of your ad in driving conversions and achieving your campaign goals.

5. Cost per Click (CPC) or Cost per Action (CPA): These metrics measure the average cost you pay for each click or action generated by your ad. It helps evaluate the efficiency and cost-effectiveness of your campaign.

6. Return on Ad Spend (ROAS): ROAS measures the revenue generated in relation to the amount spent on advertising. It determines the profitability of your ad campaigns and provides insights into the overall effectiveness of your marketing efforts.

7. View-through Rate (VTR): VTR measures the percentage of users who viewed your ad to completion without skipping it. It indicates the engagement level and appeal of your ad content.

8. Frequency: Frequency tracks the average number of times an individual user sees your ad. Monitoring frequency helps you avoid ad fatigue and ensure your message reaches the audience without becoming repetitive.

9. Audience Demographics: Analyzing the demographic data of users who engage with your ads, such as age, gender, location, and interests, provides valuable insights into your target audience's characteristics. This information helps refine your targeting and optimize future campaigns.

10. Return on Investment (ROI): ROI measures the profitability of your ad campaigns by comparing the revenue generated to the cost of advertising. It helps determine the overall success and financial impact of your marketing efforts.

11. Brand Sentiment: Assessing brand sentiment through user comments, feedback, and sentiment analysis tools provides insights into how your ads are perceived by the audience. Positive sentiment indicates a strong brand connection, while negative sentiment may require adjustments in your ad strategy.

Remember to define your key performance indicators (KPIs) based on your campaign objectives and track these metrics regularly. Monitoring and analyzing these metrics will help you evaluate the performance of your ad campaigns, make data-driven decisions, and optimize your future advertising efforts on TikTok.

Analyzing campaign data and making data-driven decisions for optimization.

Analyzing campaign data is crucial for making data-driven decisions and optimizing your advertising efforts on TikTok. Here's a step-by-step process to help you analyze your campaign data effectively:

1. Define Key Performance Indicators (KPIs): Start by identifying the key metrics that align with your campaign objectives. These could include metrics like click-through rate (CTR), conversion rate, return on ad spend (ROAS), or engagement rate. Clearly define your KPIs to guide your analysis.

2. Gather Data: Collect data from your TikTok Ads Manager or analytics tools. Ensure that you have access to relevant metrics and performance

data for your ad campaigns, such as impressions, clicks, conversions, and engagement metrics.

3. Segment Data: Break down your data into meaningful segments to gain deeper insights. Analyze data by campaign, ad group, target audience, creative variations, or other relevant dimensions. This segmentation helps you identify patterns, trends, and areas for optimization.

4. Compare Performance: Compare the performance of different campaigns, ad groups, or variations. Identify high-performing ads or segments that outperform others and understand the factors contributing to their success. Look for patterns or correlations between specific elements and performance metrics.

5. Identify Underperforming Areas: Identify underperforming ads, campaigns, or targeting segments. Look for metrics that fall below your desired benchmarks or have a lower return on investment. Pinpoint areas that need improvement or optimization.

6. Conduct A/B Testing: Use A/B testing to compare different variables or creative elements within your campaigns. Test variations in ad copy, visuals, calls-to-action, or targeting options. Analyze the performance of each variation to identify the most effective elements.

7. Analyze Audience Insights: Dig into audience demographics and behavior data to better understand your target audience. Identify characteristics of your most engaged and converting segments. Use these insights to refine your targeting and messaging for future campaigns.

8. Identify Optimization Opportunities: Based on your analysis, identify areas where you can optimize your campaigns. This could include adjusting ad targeting, refining creative elements, modifying bidding strategies, or reallocating budgets. Focus on areas that have the potential to improve your key metrics.

9. Implement Changes and Monitor Results: Apply the optimization strategies you've identified and make necessary adjustments to your

campaigns. Monitor the results closely to see if the changes have a positive impact on your performance metrics.

10. Iterate and Continuously Improve: Data-driven decision-making is an iterative process. Continuously monitor and analyze your campaign data to refine your strategies further. Identify new trends, test new ideas, and stay agile in adapting to changes in audience behavior or platform algorithms.

11. Track Long-Term Trends: Look for long-term trends in your campaign data. Analyze data over an extended period to identify seasonal patterns, audience behavior shifts, or changes in ad performance. Use this information to optimize your strategies accordingly.

By consistently analyzing your campaign data and making data-driven decisions, you can optimize your TikTok ad campaigns, improve performance, and achieve your campaign objectives more effectively. Remember to track, measure, and adapt your strategies based on the insights gained from your data analysis.

Split testing and iterating on your ad strategies for continuous improvement.

Split testing, also known as A/B testing, is a valuable method for iterating on your ad strategies and continuously improving your TikTok ad campaigns. Here's a step-by-step guide to implementing split testing for continuous improvement:

1. Define Testing Goals: Clearly define the goals of your split testing. Identify specific elements or variables you want to test, such as ad copy, visuals, targeting options, bidding strategies, or call-to-action buttons. Set measurable objectives that align with your campaign goals.

2. Create Testing Variations: Develop multiple versions of your ads, each with a single variable changed. For example, create different ad copies, use different visuals, or target different audience segments. Ensure that

you isolate and test only one variable at a time to accurately evaluate its impact on performance.

3. Allocate Test Groups: Divide your target audience into separate test groups. Assign each group to a specific variation of your ads. Make sure the test groups are similar in size and composition to ensure a fair comparison.

4. Run the Tests Simultaneously: Launch your split tests simultaneously to minimize external factors that may influence the results. Ensure that the tests run for a sufficient duration to collect statistically significant data.

5. Monitor and Measure Performance: Regularly monitor and measure the performance of each test variation. Track relevant metrics such as CTR, conversion rate, engagement rate, or ROI. Use the data to compare and evaluate the performance of each variation.

6. Draw Conclusions: Analyze the data collected from your split tests to draw conclusions. Identify the variations that outperformed others in terms of your defined KPIs. Look for statistically significant differences in performance to determine which changes had a positive impact.

7. Implement the Winning Variation: Based on your conclusions, implement the winning variation that performed the best. Use the insights gained from the split testing to optimize your overall ad strategy. This could include incorporating the successful elements into your future campaigns or scaling up the winning variation.

8. Iterate and Repeat: Split testing is an iterative process. Continuously iterate on your ad strategies by implementing new tests based on your findings. Test different variables or explore further variations to refine your approach and drive continuous improvement.

9. Monitor Long-Term Trends: Track the performance of your ads over time to identify long-term trends. Monitor how changes in variables or strategies affect the performance beyond the initial split testing phase.

Adjust your strategies accordingly to adapt to evolving trends and audience behavior.

10. Document and Learn: Keep track of the results, insights, and lessons learned from your split testing experiments. Document the changes you made, the outcomes observed, and the key takeaways. Use this knowledge to inform your future ad strategies and optimization efforts.

By consistently running split tests and iterating on your ad strategies, you can make data-driven improvements, optimize performance, and increase the effectiveness of your TikTok ad campaigns over time. Remember to stay organized, track your results, and apply the insights gained from each test to refine your advertising approach.

Chapter 7: Scaling Your TikTok Advertising Success

Strategies for scaling your ad campaigns while maintaining efficiency and cost-effectiveness.

Scaling your ad campaigns on TikTok can help you reach a larger audience and drive more significant results. However, it's important to maintain efficiency and cost-effectiveness as you scale. Here are some strategies to help you achieve that balance:

1. Optimize Your Targeting: Refine your targeting options to reach the most relevant audience for your ad campaigns. Continuously analyze the performance data and adjust your targeting parameters based on audience demographics, interests, behaviors, and engagement with your ads. By focusing on the most responsive audience segments, you can maximize efficiency and avoid wasting ad spend on irrelevant viewers.

2. Expand Your Audience: While optimizing targeting is crucial, consider expanding your audience reach by exploring new demographics or targeting options. Test different audience segments to identify untapped

opportunities. Keep an eye on emerging trends and changes in user behavior to adapt your targeting strategies accordingly.

3. Utilize Lookalike Audiences: Leverage TikTok's lookalike audience feature to reach users who share similar characteristics and behaviors with your existing customers or engaged audience. Lookalike audiences can help you expand your reach while maintaining relevance, as they are more likely to be interested in your offerings.

4. Scale Incrementally: Instead of rapidly increasing your budget or ad spend, consider scaling your campaigns incrementally. Gradually increase your budget while monitoring performance closely. This approach allows you to assess the impact of scaling on key metrics and make necessary optimizations along the way.

5. Monitor Frequency and Ad Fatigue: As you scale your campaigns, pay attention to ad frequency and potential ad fatigue. Monitor how frequently your ads are shown to individual users to avoid overexposure. High ad frequency can lead to diminishing returns and decreased engagement. Consider adjusting your campaign settings, such as frequency caps or rotation of creatives, to maintain efficiency.

6. Continuously Test and Optimize: Scaling is an opportunity to test new strategies and optimize your ad campaigns further. Implement ongoing split testing to explore different variables, such as ad copy, visuals, or calls-to-action, to identify what resonates best with your expanding audience. Data-driven optimizations allow you to improve efficiency and maximize results as you scale.

7. Leverage Automation and Bidding Strategies: Utilize TikTok's automation and bidding features to streamline campaign management and optimize cost-effectiveness. Experiment with different bidding strategies, such as target cost, target return on ad spend (ROAS), or maximize conversions, to find the approach that aligns best with your goals and budget.

8. Monitor and Adjust ROI: Continuously assess the return on investment (ROI) of your ad campaigns as you scale. Regularly track the revenue generated and compare it to your advertising costs. If the ROI starts to decline or the cost per acquisition increases significantly, revisit your strategies and make adjustments to ensure cost-effectiveness.

9. Leverage Dynamic Creative Optimization (DCO): Use TikTok's DCO feature to automatically generate and optimize ad creative variations based on user preferences and performance data. DCO can help increase engagement and conversion rates while reducing the time and effort required to manually create and test multiple ad versions.

10. Monitor Industry and Platform Trends: Stay informed about industry and TikTok platform trends to capitalize on new opportunities and adjust your strategies accordingly. Monitor changes in user behavior, emerging ad formats, or platform updates that may impact the effectiveness of your campaigns. By staying ahead of trends, you can maintain efficiency and drive cost-effective scaling.

Remember that scaling your ad campaigns requires continuous monitoring, analysis, and optimization. Regularly evaluate the performance metrics, experiment with different strategies, and adapt your approach based on data-driven insights to ensure efficient and cost-effective scaling on TikTok.

Exploring advanced features and targeting options to expand your reach.

To expand your reach on TikTok and tap into advanced features and targeting options, consider the following strategies:

1. Custom Audiences: Utilize TikTok's Custom Audiences feature to reach specific groups of users based on their interactions with your brand. You can create custom audiences using sources such as website visitors, app users, customer lists, or engagement with your TikTok content. By targeting these audiences, you can reach users who have already shown

interest in your brand, increasing the likelihood of engagement and conversions.

2. Retargeting: Implement retargeting campaigns on TikTok to re-engage users who have previously interacted with your brand. Set up retargeting pixels or SDK integration to track users who have visited your website or performed specific actions. Create ads specifically tailored to these retargeted audiences, reminding them of your brand and enticing them to take further action.

3. Interest-based Targeting: Explore interest-based targeting options on TikTok to expand your reach to users who share specific interests or behaviors relevant to your brand. TikTok offers a wide range of interest categories to choose from, allowing you to target users based on their hobbies, preferences, or other relevant affinities. This enables you to connect with audiences beyond your existing customer base and tap into new market segments.

4. Behavior-based Targeting: Take advantage of TikTok's behavior-based targeting capabilities to reach users based on their past behaviors or actions on the platform. Target users who have interacted with specific types of content, engaged with certain ad formats, or exhibited behaviors aligned with your campaign objectives. This allows you to connect with users who have shown a higher propensity for engagement and conversions.

5. Location Targeting: Refine your targeting by leveraging TikTok's location targeting options. Specify locations relevant to your business, whether it's targeting users in specific cities, regions, or countries. Location targeting helps ensure that your ads are reaching the right audience based on geographical relevance and can be particularly useful for local businesses or campaigns with specific regional targets.

6. Device and Network Targeting: Tailor your ads to specific devices or networks to optimize your reach and message delivery. Target users based on device types, such as mobile or tablet, to optimize the ad

experience for different screen sizes. You can also target users based on network types, such as Wi-Fi or mobile data, to optimize ad delivery based on connection quality and user behavior.

7. Exclusion Targeting: Use exclusion targeting to refine your ad targeting by excluding specific audiences or behaviors that may not align with your campaign goals. For example, exclude existing customers or website visitors to focus on acquiring new customers. By strategically excluding certain segments, you can allocate your budget more effectively and ensure your ads are reaching the most relevant audiences.

8. Collaborate with TikTok Creators: Leverage TikTok's Creator Marketplace to collaborate with popular content creators on the platform. Partnering with influencers and creators who align with your brand can help you tap into their established audience base and expand your reach organically. Influencer partnerships can provide an effective way to reach new audiences and generate authentic engagement.

9. Cross-Platform Promotion: Extend your reach by leveraging cross-platform promotion. Promote your TikTok ads on other social media platforms or your website to drive traffic and increase visibility. Encourage your existing audience on other channels to follow you on TikTok, creating a cross-platform presence that expands your reach and increases brand exposure.

10. Test New Ad Formats and Features: Stay up to date with the latest ad formats and features introduced by TikTok. Experiment with new formats, such as shoppable ads, augmented reality (AR) effects, or interactive elements, to engage users in innovative ways. Testing new features allows you to differentiate your brand, capture attention, and expand your reach among TikTok's diverse

Case studies of successful TikTok advertising campaigns and key takeaways.

Case Study 1: Guess Jeans - #InMyDenim Challenge

Guess Jeans launched a successful TikTok advertising campaign with the hashtag challenge #InMyDenim. They encouraged TikTok users to create and share videos of themselves transforming from casual to fashionable while wearing Guess jeans. The campaign generated massive engagement and user participation, resulting in over 38,000 user-generated videos and 5.5 billion views.

Key Takeaways:

1. Hashtag challenges can be a powerful tool for driving user engagement and brand awareness on TikTok.

2. Encouraging user-generated content can generate a sense of community and authenticity around your brand.

3. Leveraging TikTok's creative and fun culture can help capture the attention and interest of the platform's user base.

4. Partnering with influencers and popular creators can amplify the reach and impact of your campaign.

Case Study 2: Fenty Beauty - Fenty Glow Challenge

Fenty Beauty, the makeup brand created by Rihanna, launched the Fenty Glow Challenge on TikTok. The challenge invited users to showcase their natural beauty by using Fenty Beauty's Fenty Glow lip gloss. The campaign gained significant traction, generating over 3.3 million video creations and 7 billion views.

Key Takeaways:

1. Aligning your campaign with popular trends or challenges can help boost participation and engagement.

2. Leveraging user-generated content and user testimonials can build trust and authenticity for your brand.

3. Emphasizing the unique features and benefits of your product can drive interest and conversions.

4. Capitalizing on TikTok's visually-driven platform can showcase your product effectively and create a buzz around it.

Case Study 3: Chipotle - #GuacDance Challenge

Chipotle, the fast-food chain, launched the #GuacDance challenge on TikTok to celebrate National Avocado Day. The challenge encouraged users to show off their dance moves while incorporating an avocado-themed dance move. The campaign garnered over 250,000 video submissions and 430 million video starts within six days.

Key Takeaways:

1. Leveraging holidays or special events can provide a timely opportunity to engage with users and drive participation.

2. Incorporating a dance challenge can make your campaign more interactive and shareable.

3. Offering incentives or rewards, such as discounts or freebies, can incentivize participation and boost engagement.

4. Creative and playful campaigns can resonate well with TikTok's young and enthusiastic user base.

These case studies highlight the effectiveness of leveraging TikTok's unique features and culture to create engaging and successful advertising campaigns. The key takeaways include embracing user-generated content, leveraging popular trends and challenges, partnering with influencers, emphasizing product features and benefits, and tapping into the creative and fun nature of TikTok. By applying these strategies, brands can achieve significant reach, engagement, and brand exposure on the platform.

Conclusion:

"Mastering TikTok Ads: Unlocking the Power of Viral Marketing" equips you with the knowledge, strategies, and tools to leverage TikTok's immense advertising potential. By following the techniques outlined in this ebook, you can create impactful ad campaigns, drive brand awareness, and achieve remarkable results in the dynamic world of TikTok advertising. Start your journey today and unlock the power of viral marketing on TikTok!

www.ingramcontent.com/pod-product-compliance
Lightning Source LLC
Chambersburg PA
CBHW070843220526
45466CB00002B/871